HISTORY FROM OBJECTS
IN THE STREET

Karen Bryant-Mole

Wayland

HISTORY FROM OBJECTS

In The Home
Keeping Clean
At School
Toys
Clothes
In The Street

First published in 1994 by
Wayland (Publishers) Ltd
61 Western Road, Hove
East Sussex, BN3 1JD, England

© Copyright 1994 Wayland (Publishers) Ltd

Edited by Deborah Elliott
Designed by Malcolm Walker

British Library Cataloguing in Publication Data
Bryant-Mole, Karen
 In the Street. - (History From Objects Series)
 I. Title II. Series
 941

ISBN 0 7502 1021 4

Typeset by Kudos Editorial and Design Services
Printed and bound by BPC Paulton Books Ltd

Notes for parents and teachers
This book has been designed to be used on many different levels.

It can be used as a means of comparing and contrasting objects from the past with those of the present. Differences between the objects can be identified.

It can be used to look at the way designs have developed as our knowledge and technology have improved. Vehicles that were drawn by horses are now powered by engines. Goods that were sold loose, now come ready packaged. Children can consider the similarities between the objects and look at the way particular design features have been refined. The book can be used to help place objects in chronological order and to help children understand that development in design corresponds with a progression through time.

It can also be used to make deductions about the way people in the past lived their lives. Children can think about how and why the objects might have been used and who might have used them. It is designed to show children that historical objects can reveal much about the past. At the same time it links the past with the present by showing that many of the familiar objects we use today have their roots planted firmly in history.

Contents

Butcher	4
Chemist	6
Petrol station	8
Car	10
Delivery lorry	12
Draper	14
General store	16
Baker	18
Corner shop	20
Barber	22
Sweetshop	24
Bus	26
Milk deliveries	28
Glossary	30
Books to read	31
Index	32

Some of the more difficult words which appear in **bold** in the text are explained in the glossary on page 30.

Butcher

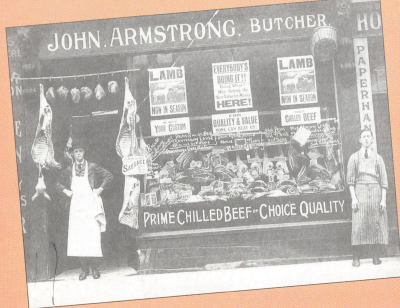

1900s
Can you see the posters that say `LAMB NOW IN SEASON'? In the past, there were only certain months of the year when you could buy lamb. Now, with modern **freezers**, we can have lamb all year round.

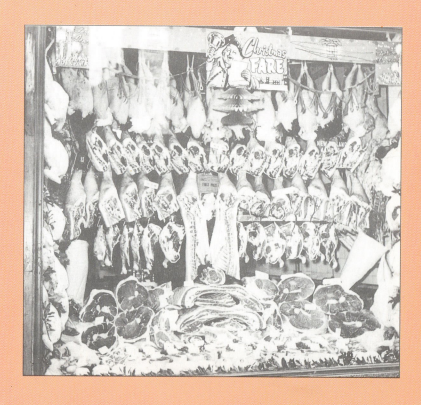

1930s
This butcher's window is packed full of **joints** of meat. If you look along the top of the window and down the sides you will see lots of turkeys. What time of year was it when this photo was taken?

1940s

This photograph was taken during the **Second World War**. Can you see that there is much less meat in the window than in the 1930s' window? People could buy only a small amount of meat each week, because there was not much food available. This was called **rationing**.

Now

There are lots of different types of meat in this butcher's window. There is pork, beef, chicken and lamb. There are joints, steaks, chops and mince. There is even **haggis**! All the meat is stored in a chilled cabinet to keep it fresh and cool.

 # Chemist

1890s

This type of chemist's shop used to be known as a pharmacy. A pharmacy was a place where medicines were made and sold. Can you see the rows and rows of bottles on the shelves? These were the **ingredients** for the medicines.

1920s

These two people are mixing together some medicines. The woman is making a medicine that can be drunk. The man is mixing a powder. He might be going to make it into pills.

1940s
Can you see the two big glass jars in the window of this chemist's shop? Lots of shops had **symbols** as well as words to tell people what sort of shop they were. These jars were the symbol for a chemist.

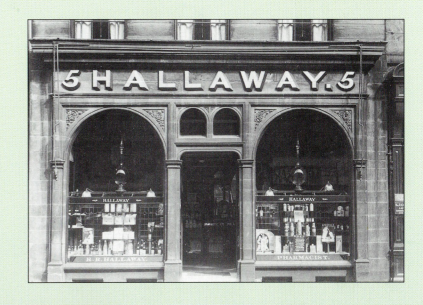

Now
Today, many of our medicines come in bottles and packets that we can just buy off the shelf. Some medicines can only be bought with a note from a doctor. This note is called a prescription.

Petrol station

1920s

Don't these petrol pumps look tall and narrow? When the customers drove into the garage, the owner would have filled up their petrol tanks for them. The owner had to use a big **lever** to pump the petrol up from tanks which were under the ground.

1950s

This petrol station sold two different **brands** of petrol. The petrol pumps look more like the ones we have today. There is also a car showroom where cars could be bought.

Now

Petrol stations sell only one brand of petrol. The customers fill up their tanks themselves. This petrol station is open all day and all night.

IN THE STREET

Car

1910s

The very first cars were often very big. Lots of cars had soft tops which could be folded back. Can you see this car's windscreen?

1930s

The first cars were usually built by hand, but by this time cars were being made in factories. This meant that cars became cheaper and more people could afford to own one.

1960s

Cars like this used a lot of petrol. The petrol they ran on had **lead** in it. As more and more people drove cars, more and more lead went into the air.

Now

All new cars can run on unleaded petrol. Unleaded petrol is cleaner than leaded petrol. It does not **pollute** the air as much.

Delivery lorry

1890s
The first **vehicles** to deliver goods to shops were horse-drawn carts. Two horses were often used as the loads were sometimes very heavy.

1940s
By now, trucks like the one in this picture were being used to deliver goods. Can you see that the part of the truck where the goods were carried had no roof? A waterproof cover was probably tied on when it rained.

Now
Some modern delivery lorries are huge. They can carry enough food in them to fill a small shop. Very big lorries often have lots of wheels.

Draper

1920s

Shops where material, or fabric, was sold used to be called drapers' shops. There are some clothes in the window of this shop which show the styles that people wore at the time.

1940s

Look at all the different rolls of fabric. Are they mostly patterned or plain? In the 1940s people usually made their clothes themselves or had their clothes made specially for them.

1950s

Look at all the patterns on the material in this shop window! Fewer people bought fabric now as it was easier to buy ready-made clothes in a clothes shop.

Now

Today, very many of the fabrics we buy are easy to wash and care for. Most of the people who buy fabric here will be making clothes for themselves or for their families.

# General store

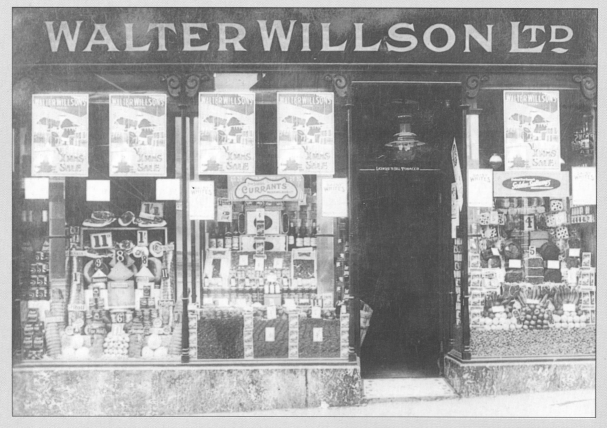

1910s
Lots of the things that were sold in this shop were stored in big boxes or jars. The customers decided how much they wanted and the shopkeeper would weigh it out and wrap it up.

1950s
This is an early self-service shop. Instead of being served by the shopkeeper, the customers walked around the shop putting their shopping in a basket.

Now
Many people shop at large supermarkets which sell lots of different things. People like them because they can do all their shopping in one shop.

Baker

1930s
Look at all the different sorts of cakes you could buy in this shop! Each cake has a label on it which tells the customers its price.

1940s
There are lots of different types of bread in this baker's window. Can you see some bread shaped like a sheaf of corn? Even today, some bakers bake bread like this at harvest-time.

Now
Many of the cakes and biscuits in this shop window have been made specially for children. Can you see some gingerbread men, some funny face cakes, some dinosaur biscuits and a clown cake?

 # Corner shop

1900s
Corner shops weren't in the centre of town but in the roads where people lived. They usually sold the sorts of things that people used every day.

1920s

There are adverts on the shop-front for some of the things that were sold in this shop. Other goods were displayed in the windows. There used to be lots and lots of corner shops.

Now

Today, corner shops still sell things that people use each day. Now, however, there are far fewer corner shops. Many people choose to shop at larger supermarkets. If the corner shopkeeper does not have enough customers, he or she has to close down.

Barber

1910s
Barbers used to shave men's beards as well as cut their hair. There are lots of hair care products in this shop. The customers could buy these to take home with them.

1950s
This young man is having his hair blow dried with a hairdryer. The hairdresser is wearing a white overall on top of his ordinary clothes.

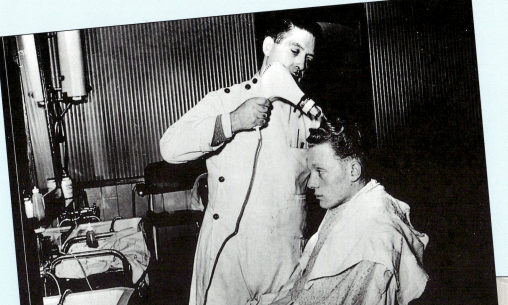

Now
The barber has different hairbrushes for different types of hair. Can you see a yellow hairdryer? Next to it are some electric clippers. But the barber's most useful tools are, as they always have been, his scissors.

Sweetshop

1890s
Almost all of the sweets in this sweetshop were stored in jars, boxes or trays. The customers could buy as much or as little as they wanted. The sweets were often wrapped in twists of paper.

1940s
This sweetshop was also a temperance bar. This meant that the customers could buy soft drinks, such as lemonade, as well as sweets.

Now

Most of today's sweets come already wrapped in their own packets. There are very few shops these days that just sell sweets. Most people buy their sweets at **newsagents** or in supermarkets.

Bus

1900s

The first buses were pulled by horses. The staircase goes up the outside of this bus. Would you have liked to sit upstairs on a rainy day?

1910s

This bus is powered by an engine. The driver's **cab** has no windows. He has only a roof for shelter. Buses used to be called omnibuses, but the word has now been shortened.

1950s

Everyone on this bus could travel undercover. Two people worked on the bus, the driver, who drove the bus, and the conductor, who collected the money.

Now

Only one person works on this bus. When passengers get on they pay the driver who gives them a ticket. He or she then drives on to the next stop.

Milk deliveries

1910s

The milk is in the two big churns on this horse-drawn cart. The milkman would have scooped out the milk from the churns and tipped it into the jugs or pails brought to him by his customers.

28

1930s

These milkmen are using a van to deliver milk. If you look at the basket that one of the men is holding, you will see that they sold milk in one **pint** and half pint bottles.

Now

This milk float is powered by a big battery which gets charged up every day. When the milkman's customers have used the milk, they rinse the bottles and put them out for him to collect the next day.

Glossary

brands particular makes of goods
cab the front part of the bus where the driver sits
freezers machines which freeze food and keep it frozen
haggis a mixture of minced meat (usually sheep's liver), oatmeal, suet and onions
ingredients what something is made of (the label on a food packet tells you all its ingredients)
joints large cuts of meat
lead a chemical found in leaded petrol which can be harmful
lever a bar which is pulled, pushed or lifted to make something work
newsagents shops which sell sweets, magazines and newspapers
pint a measurement which is about the same as half a litre
pollute make dirty
rationing when food is shared out so that everyone has a fair share
Second World War a war fought in Europe between 1939 and 1945
symbols objects or signs which mean the same as words
vehicles cars, lorries, buses and other types of transport that travel on land

Books to read

How We Used To Live, 1902-1926 by Freda Kelsall (A & C Black, 1985)
How We Used To Live, 1954-1970 by Freda Kelsall (A & C Black, 1987)
Looking Back series (Wayland, 1991)
Starting History series (Wayland, 1991)

Index

bakers' shops   18-19
barbers' shops   22-3
bus   26-7
butchers' shops   4-5

cars   10-11
car showroom   8
carts, horse-drawn   12, 28
chemists' shops   6-7
corner shops   20-21

delivery lorries   12-13
drapers' shops   14-15

garages   8
general stores   16-17

medicines   6, 7
milk floats   29

newsagents   25, 30

petrol stations   8-9
pharmacy   (see chemists' shops)

shop windows   21
supermarkets   17, 21, 25
sweetshops   24-5

trucks   13

vehicles   12, 13, 26-7, 29, 30

Acknowledgements
The photographs in this book were supplied by the following; Beamish, The North of England Open Air Museum title page, contents page, 4 (both), 5 (top), 6 (both), 7 (top), 8 (both), 10 (both), 12, 13 (top), 14 (both), 15 (top), 16, 17 (top), 18 (both), 20, 21 (top), 22, 23 (top), 24 (both), 26 (both), 28, 29 (top); Chapel Studios 5 (bottom), 7 (bottom), 9, 11, (bottom), 13 (bottom), 15 (bottom), 17 (bottom), 19, 21 (bottom), 23 (bottom), 25, 27 (bottom), 29 (bottom); Neill Bruce 11 (top), Eye Ubiquitous 27 (top).